Sushi

W9-DIO-185

Recipe	Page	Calories/piece	Classic	Easy to prepare	A little more effort	Highly decorative	A little more expensive	Refined	Vegetarian	Quick
Nigiri Sushi with Tuna	12	102	●	●						
Nigiri Sushi with Shrimp Omelet	14	241		●		●				
Nigiri Sushi with Pickled Mackerel	14	92			●			●		
Nigiri Sushi with Trout	16	94	●	●						
Nigiri Sushi with Flounder	16	75		●			●			
Nigiri Sushi with Wolf Perch	17	74	●			●				
Nigiri Sushi with Marinated Salmon	17	113				●		●		
Nigiri Sushi with Anchovies	18	79			●	●				
Nigiri Sushi with Chinese Mushrooms and Tofu	18	81						●	●	
Nigiri Sushi with Cuttlefish	20	76	●				●			
Nigiri Sushi with Scallops	20	63				●	●			
Hosomaki with Fried Salmon and Chives	24	45			●			●		
Hosomaki with Avocado and Sesame	26	35							●	●
Hosomaki with Zucchini and Radish Shoots	26	22							●	●
Hosomaki with Tuna	28	35	●							●
Hosomaki with Surimi and Arugula	28	22				●				●
Futomaki with Tofu and Shitake Mushrooms	30	61			●				●	
Futomaki with Omelet, Surimi and Carrots	30	58			●			●		
Futomaki with Radish and Smoked Trout	32	43		●				●		
Gunkan Maki with Trout Caviar	32	73	●							●
Gunkan Maki with Cream of Smoked Eel	34	82	●							●
Gunkan Maki with Mussels	34	70				●				
Ura Maki with Surimi and Avocado	38	45			●	●				
Ura Maki with Chopped Tuna	40	35			●	●				

Recipe

Table

Sushi Primer

What is sushi? Where does it come from? What is the secret of these tasty morsels and how should you eat them? This is the place to learn the sushi basics. Nigiri? Wasabi? Temaki? It's all Greek to you? In the following two pages we explain the most important terms of the sushi kitchen.

What is Sushi?

In the beginning, sushi was just "vinegar-soured rice." Today sushi means a combination of special, sticky sushi rice with other ingredients, principally raw fish.

The Invention of Sushi

Centuries ago in Southeast Asia, fish and mussels were pickled with brine, and rice was placed on top of them to keep them in the liquid. The seafood was thus kept out of the air and preserved, but in those days the rice was thrown away. Later the rice was mixed with vinegar, and as a result the fish became tender sooner, and the rice remained edible.

We owe the real invention of sushi as we know it to traveling merchants from Southeast Asia, who were probably the first to offer raw fish on top of a ball of sour rice.

The basic ingredients for classic sushi: vinegar rice, raw fish and nori leaves

Countless Varieties

When we talk of sushi, we usually mean nigiri sushi—this miniature art form of pressed rice with a slice of raw fish. But there's no need to put a limit on your creativity. Why not try sushi with young herring and spring onion, with mozzarella and tomatoes or with fried breast of duck? Admittedly, these new ideas may shock fans of traditional sushi—in reality sushi is part of Japanese culture and not just the idea of putting raw fish on top of rice. So don't think of this book as a substitute for the years of training one needs to become a true sushi chef, but rather as a western interpretation of a basic culinary idea with which you can have a lot of fun. Whether a traditional or brand new recipe, each step of preparation is carefully described, and with a little bit of practice it's as easy as pie.

Tasty and Healthy

Sushi isn't just delicious; it's good for you too. It is full of valuable nutrients, while being low in calories and fat. Fish and shellfish contain highly nutritious proteins, vitamins and minerals. Rice and green vegetables contain carbohydrates, fiber, vitamins and a great variety of minerals, and seaweed is rich in iodine.

How to Enjoy Sushi

You Can't Do It Without...

Sushi is always accompanied by three things: soy sauce, wasabi and gari (pickled ginger).

Put a drop of soy sauce into a small, flat bowl. Then, according to how hot you want it, add a bit of wasabi paste to the sauce. The paste is made of green Japanese horseradish and is super hot. Dip your sushi in this sauce—but just a little, so as not to smother the delicate fish flavor with the salty-hot flavor of the soy and wasabi.

Gari—sweet and sour slices of vinegar-pickled ginger—are eaten between the different pieces of sushi to cleanse the palate.

With a Fork?

Sushi can be eaten either with your fingers or with chopsticks. The only exceptions to this rule are temaki sushi—always finger-food—and sashimi, which is eaten only with chopsticks. Sushi is always eaten in one mouthful, because any attempt to bite into a piece means sauce on your shirt. Temaki cones are again the exception here, because you can bite into them with no worries of spilling.

Drink This

The authentic drinks that accompany sushi are green tea or sake—Japanese rice wine. Sake should be heated in hot water and enjoyed lukewarm. Beer and mineral water also go very well with sushi.

Morsels, rolls, cylinders and cones—the classics

Nigiri sushi
Sushi's prototype: fish on top, rice below. The fish, shrimp or other delicacy is fixed to a shaped rice-ball with wasabi paste. Nigiri sushi are always served in pairs.

Maki sushi rolls
Inside is the filling, then comes the rice, and around the outside, a leaf of seaweed. The small hosomaki-rolls have one or two ingredients in the filling— 1 roll makes 6 pieces. The thick futomaki-rolls contain 3 to 5 ingredients and are usually cut into 8 portions.

Gunkan maki
Small shapes with soft filling: a base of rice with a leaf of seaweed around it to form a cup, filled with caviar and other soft ingredients, or sometimes with chunkier fillings.

Temaki
Little "ice-cream cones" made of seaweed, filled with sushi rice and lots of other ingredients.

Ura maki
"Inside-out" rolls, with filling in the middle, then seaweed, and the rice on the outisde.

Other sushi shapes and sushi ingredients

Sashimi
Sushi without the rice: pieces of raw fish fillet with green vegetables elaborately prepared on plates or sushi boards.

Chirashi
Usually warm sushi rice prepared with one or several fishy ingredients in a bowl.

Pickled ginger (gari)
"Gari" is short for gari shoga (pickled ginger). You can buy it ready to use from Asian food stores.

Wasabi
Very hot Japanese horseradish, almost impossible to acquire fresh, but available as paste ready to use in a tube, or as powder to be mixed with water. Stir 2 tsp wasabi powder with 3 tsp water and let it swell slightly.

Vinegar water (tezu)
So that the rice sticks only where it's supposed to and not to your fingers, mix 1 cup of water with 4 tbs of rice-vinegar and moisten your hands repeatedly while you are forming sushi. To cut maki sushi, wet the knife between cuts with tezu.

More ingredients for the sushi kitchen

Japanese soy sauce (shoyu)
Like all soy sauces, shoyu is made from fermented soybeans, but it is not as salty as Chinese soy sauce.

Mirin
Sweet Japanese rice-wine, used in cooking.

Dashi
Basic fish broth; buy ready-to-use from Asian food stores.

Nori
Dried, pressed seaweed used as wrapping for sushi rolls. You can buy nori leaves pre-roasted, or lightly toast them yourself over a gas flame or electric burner until they smell good and are crisp.

Kombu
Dried seaweed added as flavoring in cooking rice.

All these typical sushi kitchen basics can be found in Asian food stores or in well-stocked supermarkets on the gourmet shelves or in the Asian ingredients section. You can also usually find Asian ingredients in the food section(s) of large warehouse stores.

Roll-your-own sushi

Invite your guests to a sushi party, but with a twist: Your friends will roll and form—you just handle the preparations!

Don't be afraid, sushi is much easier than you think, and with a little bit of practice you will soon craft your favorite individual sushi. Everyone gets his or her own bamboo rolling mat and a little bowl of vinegar water to wet their fingers, and off they go. With temaki and company the evening will be more fun than with the old faithful fondue, and with the leftover fillings you can put together some big futomaki for when your guests come back.

By the way: if it ever really happens that sushi is left over, just wrap it in clear film and put it in a cool place. Not in the fridge though, because it's too cold, and they go hard. It's best to enjoy your sushi as soon as possible, because the fish has to be as fresh as it can be.

Basic Sushi Rice Recipe

For perfect sushi you should use special Japanese round-grain rice.

Unlike long-grain or parboiled rice, this rice remains sticky after boiling—this usually undesired quality is a basic necessity for sushi because you can only form it well with sticky rice.

Japanese round-grain rice can be found, like the other ingredients of the sushi kitchen, in any Asian food store. If sushi hankerings come over you on a Sunday or holiday, you might try milk-rice or Italian risotto from the cupboard; but remember, only in times of dire need.

The amount of rice specified in this basic recipe is enough for two of the book's sushi recipes—for example for eight nigiri pieces and 24 pieces of hosomaki. How many friends you may feed with it depends on the type of meal and the hunger of your guests. If you serve sushi as an appetizer, you will be OK with two different kinds of nigiri at two pieces per person, or with one type of nigiri at two pieces and half a hosomaki roll (3 pieces) per person.

If you want to prepare a pure sushi menu, count three to four kinds of nigiri at two pieces per person plus a whole hosomaki roll each.

Ingredients:

8 oz sushi rice

1 1/4 cups water

1 small piece kombu (about 1 1/2 inch x 1 1/2 inch) according to taste

2 tbs rice vinegar

2 tbs sugar

1 tsp salt

Prep time: 45 minutes

Total approx: 927 calories 19g protein/5 g fat/202 g carbohydrates

1 Clean the rice with cold running water until the water runs clear. Let it drain well.

2 Put the rice, kombu and water in a saucepan and let the rice swell slightly. Bring it to the boil and let it boil for 2 minutes at high heat. Then cover with a lid and let it simmer for 10 minutes at the lowest heat, until the rice is just cooked but no more.

3 Take the pan from the stove, remove the lid, and let the rice cool for 10 minutes, covered only with a damp cloth.

4 In the meantime, heat the vinegar, sugar and salt in a small pot and stir until the sugar and salt dissolve. Remove from heat, and allow to cool.

5 Empty the rice into a flat bowl (traditionally a wooden bowl is used, but a stoneware bowl works well too). Take out the seaweed and mix the rice with the vinegar mixture using a wooden spatula.

6 To cool the rice down quickly, make holes in it and fan with the wooden spatula . The rice should be cool in 10 minutes. If you feel open to trying an alternative to this traditional method, just use a hairdryer set to "cold"—it works perfectly. Don't put the rice in the fridge or stir it too much during the cooling because it will go dry.

7 Cover the cooled sushi rice with a damp kitchen towel until you use it, so that it doesn't dry out.

Nigiri Sushi

If the subject is sushi, most people think of nigiri sushi; the sushi classic in which fish crowns an oval cake of rice.

It is easy to understand why this simple combination established itself as a Japanese national dish: Japan is surrounded by the sea, containing countless varieties of delicious edible treasures, and her staple food has always been rice.

There is Art in Simplicity

Although it takes years for a Japanese apprentice chef to rise to the category of itamae—a sushi master—newcomers can easily prepare perfect nigiri sushi morsels with just a little practice. Both the aroma of its natural ingredients and its minimalist aesthetics make nigiri sushi a highly decorative, yet simple delight.

Minimalism of the first order: to prepare nigiri sushi only a few, carefully selected ingredients are needed.

Ingredients

The basic ingredients for classic nigiri sushi are rice, raw fish and wasabi. In Japanese kitchens, great emphasis is placed on the image—the food's mouth-watering appearance. Think of the different colors of sushi's fish toppings: red flesh of tuna and white flesh of wolf perch; pink-orange salmon, or the blue shimmering skins of sardine and mackerel.

A little wasabi between rice and topping gives the right spicy kick. On the side, soy sauce and pickled ginger are musts. Dip only the fish part of the sushi in the soy sauce, otherwise the rice will soak up too much of it and overpower the flavor of the fish. This also prevents the rice from falling apart. Pickled ginger serves to neutralize the taste between the different sushi morsels and refresh the palate.

Variations on a Theme

Nigiri sushi means more than just traditional raw fish. The rule is: if it tastes good, use it. In this chapter, alongside the classics, you will find nigiri sushi made with omelet, mussels or squid, a vegetarian recipe, and a variation with pickled salmon.

If you are feeling adventurous, you can vary the shape of the sushi, forming flatter or rounder balls. Another variant of nigiri sushi, established long ago in Japan, is gunkan maki. You will find that recipe on page 23.

Buying and Preparing the Fish

Fresh fish smells pleasantly of seaweed— it should never smell strongly of fish. The flesh should be relatively firm and will bounce back when pressed with your finger.

The raw fish fillet used for sushi should not contain any bones. Take out all the bones—the smallest of them may be removed with a pair of tweezers or kitchen pliers used only for food. You can get special tweezers at the fish market or in household goods stores.

Serving...

Sushi should not be eaten warmer than room temperature. Sushi that has been prepared beforehand should be kept in the refrigerator and taken out just before serving. Best of all is to prepare sushi just before eating.

...and Eating Right

Sushi belongs to the Japanese delicacies eaten simply with your fingers. Just take the piece between thumb and index finger, dip the fish into the soy sauce, and then pop it in your mouth. Try sushi as finger-food for your next party!

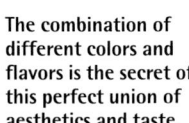

The combination of different colors and flavors is the secret of this perfect union of aesthetics and taste.

Nigiri Sushi with Tuna

● Classic
● East to prepare

Yields 8 pieces:

5–6 oz fresh tuna fillet
2 tsp wasabi powder
vinegar water
1/2 recipe of pre-prepared sushi rice (see page 8)
To serve:
soy sauce
pickled ginger

Prep time: 30 minutes

Per piece: 102 calories
5g protein/3 g fat/13 g carbohydrates

1 Dry the tuna with a cloth and trim to make straight edges. Then cut the fillet with a sharp knife into 8 equal pieces, about 1 inch x 2 inches. Cuts should be made crosswise to the white fibers, on a slight diagonal.

2 Stir the wasabi powder together with 3 tsp water and let it swell slightly. Spread a little of the wasabi paste in the center of each piece of fish.

3 Moisten your hands with vinegar water and form the sushi rice into 8 oval cakes. To prevent the rice from sticking to your hands as you form the cakes, wet your hands repeatedly with the vinegar water. Also be careful not to press the rice too hard, because this will affect its delicate flavor.

4 Take a piece of tuna in your left hand, with the wasabi side facing up. Place a rice cake on top and press down with your thumb.

5 Move the sushi to your right hand as you turn it over. Press the tuna first from above and then from the sides to obtain a regular shape, with the rice and tuna clinging together.

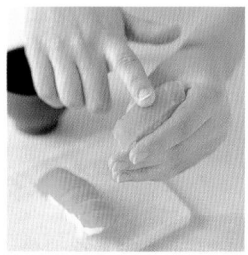

Finally, shape the sushi by squeezing with your index finger and thumb, giving it the typical nigiri sushi form.

6 Assemble and form the rest of the sushi in the same way. Arrange the sushi rice-side-down in pairs, in a decorative manner on a plate or classic sushi board. Serve with soy sauce, pickled ginger and the remaining wasabi paste.

TIP!

Tuna is not just tuna! Connoisseurs and good fish markets distinguish between the cuts: otoro, chutoro, and akami.

Otoro, the most sought-after cut of tuna, comes from the belly. It is especially light, rich in fat, and expensive.

Less expensive, lighter in color and not as rich in fat is chutoro, which is also cut from the belly region.

Akami is the word for the deep red, low-fat cut from the mid-dorsal area.

Nigiri Sushi with Shrimp Omelet

● Easy to prepare
● Highly decorative

Yields 8 pieces:

2 oz raw, peeled shrimp
1/4 cup instant dashi (fish broth)
1 tsp soy sauce
2 tbs sugar
2 tbs mirin
1 pinch salt
5 eggs
1 tbs vegetable oil
1/2 toasted nori leaf
2 tsp wasabi powder
vinegar water
1/2 recipe of pre-prepared sushi rice (see page 8)

To serve:
soy sauce
pickled ginger

Prep time: 45 minutes

Per piece: 241 calories
6g protein/5g fat/17g carbohydrates

1 Wash and dry the shrimp, and chop very finely. Mix the dashi, soy sauce, sugar, mirin and salt until the sugar and salt are dissolved. Add eggs and shrimp and stir well, but avoid making bubbles in the mixture.

2 Heat the oil in a small, non-stick frying pan (about 6 inches in diameter), put the mixture in and let it cook over a low flame for about 15 minutes.

3 Allow the omelet to cool and cut it into 8 rectangles about 1 inch x 2 inches each. Cut the nori leaf into 8 strips, 1/2 inch wide. Stir the wasabi powder together with 3 tsp of water and let it swell slightly. Spread a little of the wasabi paste on each piece of omelet.

4 Moisten your hands with vinegar water and form the sushi rice into 8 oval cakes. Take a piece of omelet in your left hand, with the wasabi side facing up. Place a rice cake on top and press down with your thumb. Continue forming the sushi as described on page 12.

5 Turn the sushi over and wrap it in the middle with a strip of nori, fixing the end of the strip with a small amount of vinegar. Serve with soy sauce, pickled ginger and the remaining wasabi paste.

Nigiri Sushi with Pickled Mackerel

● A little more effort
● Subtle and refined

Yields 8 pieces:

5-6 oz fresh mackerel fillet, with skin
3 tbs salt
1 lime
5 tbs rice vinegar
2 tbs mirin
2 tsp sugar
2 tsp wasabi powder
vinegar water
1/2 recipe of pre-prepared sushi rice (see page 8)

To serve:
soy sauce
pickled ginger

Prep time: 30 minutes plus 4 to 6 hours for pickling

Per piece: 92 calories
5g protein/2g fat/13g carbohydrates

1 Dry the mackerel fillet and remove any remaining bones. Rub with the salt and place in a cool spot for 3 to 5 hours. Then rinse off the salt with running water, and dry.

2 Wash the lime, dry it and cut 4 very thin slices from the middle. Halve the slices and set aside. Squeeze the remaining lime and mix the juice with the rice vinegar, mirin and sugar until the sugar dissolves.

3 Place the fish fillet in a flat dish, cover with the marinade, and let it stand for about 1 hour, turning over occasionally. Dry the fish, peel away the skin and use a sharp knife to cut the fillet on a diagonal into 8 even pieces.

4 Stir the wasabi powder together with 3 tsp of water and let it swell slightly. Spread a little of the wasabi paste in the center of each piece of fish.

5 Moisten your hands with vinegar water and form the sushi rice into 8 oval cakes.

6 Take a piece of fish in your left hand, with the wasabi side facing up. Place a rice cake on top and press down with your thumb.

7 Continue forming the sushi as described on page 12.

8 Assemble and form the rest of the sushi in the same way. Arrange the sushi, decorate with the lime slices, and serve with soy sauce, pickled ginger and the remaining wasabi paste.

**In the foreground:
Nigiri Sushi with
Shrimp Omelet
In the background:
Nigiri Sushi with
Pickled Mackerel**

Nigiri Sushi with Trout

- Classic
- Easy to prepare

Yields 8 pieces:

5–6 oz fresh trout fillet
2 tsp wasabi powder
vinegar water
1/2 recipe of pre-prepared sushi rice (see page 8)
To serve:
soy sauce
pickled ginger

Prep time: 30 minutes

Per piece: 94 calories
6g protein/1g fat/13g carbohydrates

1 Dry the fish, remove any remaining bones and trim to make straight edges. Cut the fish on a slight diagonal into 8 nearly-equal pieces of about 1 inch x 2 inches. Stir the wasabi powder with 3 tsp water and let it swell slightly. Spread a little of the wasabi paste in the center of each piece of fish.

2 Moisten your hands with a little vinegar water and form the sushi rice into 8 oval cakes. Take a piece of trout in your left hand, with the wasabi side facing up. Place a rice cake on top and press down with your thumb. Continue forming the sushi as described on page 12.

3 Assemble and form the rest of the sushi in the same way. Arrange the sushi and serve with soy sauce, pickled ginger and the remaining wasabi paste.

Nigiri Sushi with Flounder

- Easy to prepare
- A bit more expensive

Yields 8 pieces:

5–6 oz fresh flounder fillet
2 tsp wasabi powder
vinegar water
1/2 recipe of pre-prepared sushi rice (see page 8)
To serve:
soy sauce
pickled ginger

Prep time: 30 minutes

Per piece: 75 calories
5g protein/1g fat/13g carbohydrates

1 Dry the fish, remove any remaining bones and trim to make straight edges. Cut the fillet in half lengthwise, and then cut each half into 4 pieces about 1 inch x 2 inches each.

2 Stir the wasabi powder together with 3 tsp water and let it swell slightly. Spread a little of the wasabi paste in the center of each piece of fish.

3 Moisten your hands with vinegar water and form the sushi rice into 8 oval cakes. Take a piece of fish in your left hand, with the wasabi side facing up. Place a rice cake on top and press down with your thumb. Continue forming the sushi as described on page 12.

4 Assemble and form the rest of the sushi in the same way. Arrange the sushi and serve with soy sauce, pickled ginger and the remaining wasabi paste.

Nigiri Sushi with Wolf Perch

● Classic
● Highly decorative

Yields 8 pieces:

5–6 oz fresh wolf
perch fillet
2 tsp wasabi powder
vinegar water
1/2 **recipe of pre-prepared
sushi rice (see page 8)**
To serve:
soy sauce
pickled ginger

Prep time: 30 minutes

Per piece: 74 calories
5g protein/1g fat/13g
carbohydrates

1 Dry the fish, remove
remaining bones and
trim to make straight
edges. Cut the fillet on
a slight diagonal into
8 pieces of about 1 inch
x 2 inches each.

2 Stir the wasabi
powder together with
3 tsp water and let it
swell slightly. Spread
a little of the wasabi
paste in the center of
each piece of fish.

3 Moisten your hands
with vinegar water and
form the sushi rice into
8 oval cakes. Take a
piece of fish in your left
hand, with the wasabi
side facing up. Place a
rice cake on top and
press down with your
thumb. Continue
forming the sushi as
described on page 12.

4 Assemble and form
the rest of the sushi in
the same way. Arrange
the sushi and serve
with soy sauce, pickled
ginger and the remaining
wasabi paste.

Nigiri Sushi with Marinated Salmon

● Highly decorative
● Refined

Yields 8 pieces:

5–6 oz marinated salmon
2 tsp wasabi powder
vinegar water
1/2 **recipe of pre-prepared
sushi rice (see page 8)**
To serve:
soy sauce
pickled ginger

Prep time: 30 minutes

Per piece: 113 calories
7g protein/4g fat/13g
carbohydrates

1 Dry the salmon,
remove any remaining
bones and trim to make
straight edges. Cut the
fillet on a slight diagonal
into 8 pieces of about
1 inch x 2 inches each.

2 Stir the wasabi
powder together with
3 tsp water and let it
swell slightly. Spread
a little of the wasabi
paste in the center of
each piece of fish.

3 Moisten your hands
with vinegar water
and form the sushi rice
into 8 oval cakes. Take
a piece of fish in your
left hand, with the
wasabi side facing up.
Place a rice cake on top
and press down with
your thumb. Continue
forming the sushi as
described on page 12.

4 Assemble and form
the rest of the sushi in
the same way. Arrange
the sushi and serve with
soy sauce, pickled ginger
and the remaining
wasabi paste.

Nigiri Sushi with Anchovies

● A little more effort
● Highly decorative

Yields 8 pieces:

8 fresh anchovies
2 tbs salt
1 piece of ginger about the size of a chestnut
5 tbs rice vinegar
2 tbs mirin
2 tsp sugar
2 tsp wasabi powder
vinegar water
1/2 recipe of pre-prepared sushi rice (see page 8)
To serve:
soy sauce
pickled ginger

Prep time: 30 minutes
plus 45 minutes for pickling

Per piece: 79 calories
3g protein/1g fat/15g
carbohydrates

1 Wash the anchovies thoroughly and cut away the head and fins. Remove the backbone without separating the fillets. Dry the fish, sprinkle the salt on them, and let them pickle for 15 minutes. Then wash away the salt under cold running water and dry the anchovies with a kitchen cloth.

2 Peel the ginger and grate it very finely. Mix it with the rice vinegar, mirin and sugar until the sugar is dissolved. Put the anchovies in a flat dish, pour the ginger marinade over them, and let them pickle for 30 minutes, turning occasionally. Remove and dry the anchovies again and score their skin on a diagonal with a sharp knife.

3 Stir the wasabi powder together with 3 tsp water and let it swell slightly. Spread a little of the wasabi paste on the underside of each anchovy.

4 Moisten your hands with vinegar water and form the sushi rice into 8 oval cakes. Take a piece of fish in your left hand, with the wasabi side facing up. Place a rice cake on top and press down with your thumb. Continue forming the sushi as described on page 12.

5 Assemble and form the rest of the sushi in the same way. Arrange the sushi and serve with soy sauce, pickled ginger and the remaining wasabi paste.

Nigiri Sushi with Chinese Mushrooms and Tofu

● Refined
● Vegetarian

Yields 8 pieces:

4 oz crimini (brown) mushrooms
1 tbs vegetable oil
1 tbs soy sauce
1 tbs mirin
2 oz hard tofu
1 scallion
2 tsp wasabi powder
1/2 toasted nori leaf
vinegar water
1/2 recipe of pre-prepared sushi rice (see page 8)
To serve:
soy sauce
pickled ginger

Prep time: 30 minutes

Per piece: 81 calories
2g protein/2g fat/14g
carbohydrates

1 Clean the mushrooms and cut them into slices. Heat the oil and fry the mushrooms lightly. Remove and place in a flat dish with the soy sauce and mirin, and let them pickle. Cut the tofu into 8 equal pieces. Remove the tops and base of the scallion, wash it and cut it into slender rings.

2 Stir the wasabi powder together with 3 tsp water and let it swell slightly. Cut the nori leaf into 8 strips about 1/2 inch wide.

3 Moisten your hands with vinegar water. Form the sushi rice into 8 oval cakes and put a little of the wasabi paste onto each of them. Put one piece of tofu and some mushroom slices onto each rice cake. Wrap each piece in the middle with a strip of nori, affixing the end of the strip with a bit of vinegar water.

4 Sprinkle the sushi with the scallion rings and serve with soy sauce, pickled ginger and the remaining wasabi paste.

> ┌─ TIP! ─┐
>
> This sushi will be even tastier if you use smoked tofu.

Nigiri Sushi with Chinese Mushrooms and Tofu on the left
Nigiri Sushi with Anchovies on the right

Nigiri Sushi with Cuttlefish

● Classic
● A little more expensive

Yields 8 pieces:

8 oz fresh, cleaned
cuttlefish tubes
2 tsp wasabi powder
vinegar water
1/2 recipe of pre-prepared
sushi rice (see page 8)
To serve:
soy sauce
pickled ginger

Prep time: 30 minutes

Per piece: 76 calories
5g protein/1g fat/13g
carbohydrates

1 Open the cuttlefish's body lengthwise with a knife and dry it with a kitchen cloth. Then cut it as evenly as possible into 8 pieces of about 1 inch x 2 inches. Score each piece several times along its length.

2 Stir the wasabi powder together with 3 tsp water and let it swell slightly. With your finger, put a little of the wasabi paste on the smooth side of each piece of cuttlefish.

3 Moisten your hands with vinegar water and form the sushi rice into 8 oval cakes.

4 Take a piece of fish in your left hand, with the wasabi side facing up. Place a rice cake on top and press down with your thumb. Continue forming the sushi as described on page 12.

5 Assemble and form the rest of the sushi in the same way. Arrange the sushi decoratively and serve with soy sauce, pickled ginger and the remaining wasabi paste.

TIP!

You can boil the cuttlefish for 3 minutes in water before using if you prefer to enjoy it cooked.

Nigiri Sushi with Scallops

● Highly decorative
● A little more pricey

Yields 8 pieces:

4 fresh scallops (thawed,
previously frozen scallops
can work as an alternative)
2 thin slices of lemon
1/2 toasted nori leaf
2 tsp wasabi powder
vinegar water
1/2 recipe of pre-prepared
sushi rice (see page 8)
miso (soy bean paste)
To serve:
soy sauce
pickled ginger

Prep time: 30 minutes

Per piece: 63 calories
2g protein/1g fat/13g
carbohydrates

1 Only the white flesh of the scallops is used (see tip). Wash the scallops, dry them and cut them in two.

2 Quarter each lemon slice. Cut the nori leaf into 8 strips about 1/2 inch wide. Stir the wasabi powder together with 3 tsp water and let it swell slightly.

3 With your finger put a little of the wasabi paste onto each piece of scallop.

4 Moisten your hands with vinegar water and form the sushi rice into 8 oval cakes.

5 Take a piece of scallop in your left hand, with the wasabi side facing up. Place a rice cake on top and press down with your thumb.

6 Turn the sushi over and move it to your right hand. Carefully press it from above and from the sides into a regular shape (see page 12). Put a piece of lemon on top and wrap each sushi piece in the middle with a strip of nori, affixing the end of the strip with a small amount of vinegar water.

7 Assemble and form the rest of the sushi in the same way. Arrange the sushi decoratively on a plate or classic sushi board and add some miso. Serve with soy sauce, pickled ginger and the remaining wasabi paste.

TIPS!

The orange-colored roe-sac of the scallop is not used in this recipe. This is good news for the cook who can fry up this little delicacy in butter. You can also prepare a sushi-variant with both the white flesh and the roe-sac: In a broth of 1/2 cup of water, 5 tbs soy sauce, 5 tsp mirin and 2 tbs sugar, poach both flesh and roe-sac over very low heat. Take out the white flesh after about 5 seconds, and let the roe-sac pickle for another 3 minutes before removing. Cut both into slices and place on top of the rice cakes.

In the foreground:
Nigiri Sushi with Cuttlefish
In the background:
Nigiri Sushi with Scallops

Maki Sushi

These rolls, also known as nori maki sushi, are made by placing sushi rice on top of a roasted nori leaf, the filling in the middle, and finally rolling it all together with the help of a small mat made of bamboo pins (makisu).

Roll Playing

Afterwards, the roll is cut into even slices, usually six. You can cut them into more pieces though, and use them as an appetizer. Maki sushi rolls seem very "Japanese" to Westerners, and impress guests to no end. Although they seem like very extravagant and complicated delicacies, they are actually quick and easy to prepare.

Traditional — or Freestyle?

With maki-sushi, once again the sky's the limit for creativity. Just taste the different rolls! Don't skip the classic filling made of tuna, avocado and cucumber, but these tidbits may also be filled with crab, skinless peppers or other green vegetables. The main thing is to make sure the ingredients are fresh. In the springtime you can use herbs, and in summer, succulent sweet peas.

If you roll them carefully and firmly, maki-sushi may be cut with a sharp knife without problems.

Maki Sushi Forms

Hosomaki

The small hosomaki are rolled with half of a nori leaf (the nori leaves on the market are all the same size) and cut into 6 regular pieces.

Hosomaki are ideal when your guests are vegetarians, because they can be prepared just as well without fish. The little rolls taste great with a filling made only of green vegetables, and they look simply mouthwatering.

Futomaki

The thicker maki sushi rolls are called futomaki. They are prepared with a whole nori leaf and contain 3 to 5 ingredients in the filling. According to legend, futomaki were born because sushi chefs made their own big rolls with the leftovers after work. Today this delicacy has nothing to do with leftovers; here, too, freshness is the last word in good taste. The big sushi pieces impress most when the filling has an attractive combination of colors. Don't just fill the rolls with cucumber, avocado and white fish, but play with the color of each ingredient! You might discover unsuspected artistic talent...

Gunkan Maki

Anyone who has tried maki variations with different fillings, and those who are curious about other ways sushi can look and taste, should try gunkan maki. The specialty of this sushi variety is that here you can use soft fillings, impossible to roll into standard maki. This characteristic allows for much more leeway in the selection of ingredients, taste directions and colors. Just as with nigiri sushi,

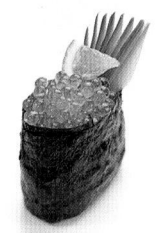

you first form an oval rice cake, which serves as the base. Around it you wrap a specially cut nori leaf to form a vertical cylinder. You can now put soft ingredients like caviar, fish cream or sea urchin roe into the opening.

Ura Maki

Another special form of maki sushi rolls is ura maki. This is explained in detail in the following chapter (page 36).

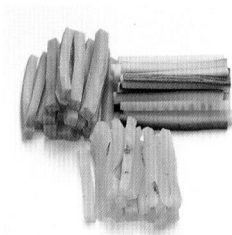

Tips and Tricks

Prep

If you don't have a bamboo mat, you can try extra strong aluminum foil as an alternative, just moisten it thoroughly with vinegar-water before rolling.

Check that the rice is at room temperature. If it is too hot, the nori leaves will go soft; too cold, and the rice won't stick together.

Eating

Eat maki sushi as soon as possible, because the nori leaves—crisp when they are fresh—will eventually soften.

Hosomaki with Fried Salmon

● A little more effort
● Refined

Yields 24 pieces:

1 bunch chives
2 tsp wasabi powder
2 tbs soy sauce
1 tbs mirin
1 tsp rice vinegar
1 tsp sugar
8 oz fresh salmon fillet with skin
flour for dusting
2 tbs vegetable oil
1 roasted nori leaf, cut into 2 halves
vinegar water
½ recipe of pre-prepared sushi rice (see page 8)
To serve:
soy sauce
pickled ginger

Prep time: 40 minutes
plus 30 minutes for pickling

Per piece: 45 calories
2g protein/2g fat/5g
carbohydrates

1 Wash the chives and dry with a cloth. Stir the wasabi powder together with 3 tsp of water and let it swell slightly.

2 For the marinade: mix soy sauce, mirin, rice vinegar and sugar into a flat dish until the sugar dissolves. Remove any remaining bones in the salmon and place it into the marinade,

cover and let it marinate for 30 minutes in the refrigerator.

3 Dry the marinated salmon with a cloth and dust lightly with flour. Heat the oil in a non-stick frying pan and fry the salmon for about 2 minutes with the skin side down, until crisp. Take it out of the pan, dab off the excess fat, and cut it with a sharp knife, lengthwise into strips.

4 Place one piece of nori leaf with the smooth side down on the bamboo rolling mat, so that the edge of the leaf is flush with the edge of the mat. Moisten your hands with vinegar water and place the sushi rice about ¼ inch thick on the nori leaf. Leave a border of nori leaf free on each side.

5 Make a small hollow along the middle of the rice for the filling, and put a bit of wasabi paste in it. Place several chives and one piece of salmon over the wasabi paste.

6 Lift the bamboo rolling mat and roll the nori leaf, rice and filling gently into a roll. Make sure that the filling remains in the center of the roll and that the roll is sufficiently hard.

7 Press the rice in at the open ends and place the roll with the loose end of the nori leaf facing down on a cutting board. Moisten a sharp knife with vinegar water and cut

the roll in half. Place the two halves side-by-side and cut into 3 pieces of the same length.

8 Repeat the process for the remaining nori leaves, rolling and cutting as described above. Arrange the sushi decoratively, and serve with soy sauce, pickled ginger and the remaining wasabi paste.

Hosomaki with Avocado and Sesame

● Vegetarian
○ Quick

Yields 24 pieces:

4 tsp sesame seeds
1/2 ripe avocado
1 tbs rice vinegar
2 tsp wasabi powder
1 roasted nori leaf,
cut into 2 halves
vinegar water
1/2 recipe of pre-prepared
sushi rice (see page 8)
To serve:
soy sauce
pickled ginger

Prep time: 20 minutes

Per piece: 35 calories
1g protein/2g fat/4g
carbohydrates

1 Roast the sesame seeds in a pan without oil until they are golden. Set them aside.

2 Peel the avocado half, cut the flesh lengthwise into 8 regular slices and sprinkle them with vinegar. Stir the wasabi powder with 3 tsp water and let it swell slightly.

3 Using your bamboo rolling mat (see how on page 24), form 4 hosomaki rolls out of the prepared ingredients.

4 Moisten a sharp knife with vinegar water, cut each roll in half and then cut the halves into 3 pieces of the same size, cutting either diagonally or straight. Arrange the sushi with the cut side facing up and serve with soy sauce, pickled ginger and the remaining wasabi paste.

TIP!

As a filling for vegetarian hosomaki, carrot and cucumber strips are very suitable (made from peeled cucumber minus the seeds and sliced thinly). Peel and cut the carrots into strips about 1/4 inch wide, and boil for 1 minute in a mixture of 5 tbs mirin, 1 tbs rice vinegar, 1/2 tsp sugar and a pinch of salt. Allow them to cool down in the broth.

Hosomaki with Zucchini and Radish Shoots

● Vegetarian
○ Quick

Yields 24 pieces:

2 oz radish shoots
1 piece zucchini
(about 4 inches long)
2 tsp wasabi powder
1 roasted nori leaf,
cut into 2 halves
vinegar water
1/2 recipe of pre-prepared
sushi rice (see page 8)
To serve:
soy sauce
pickled ginger

Prep time: 20 minutes

Per piece: 22 calories
1g protein/<1g fat/5g
carbohydrates

1 Wash the radish shoots, let them drain, and dab them dry.

2 Cut the zucchini into halves or quarters, remove the seeds, and cut the zucchini pieces into evenly sized strips.

3 Stir the wasabi powder with 3 tsp water and let it swell slightly.

4 Using your bamboo rolling mat (see how on page 24), form 4 hosomaki rolls out of the prepared ingredients.

5 Moisten a sharp knife with vinegar water, cut each roll in half and then cut the halves into 3 pieces of the same size, cutting either diagonally or straight.

6 Arrange the sushi with the cut side facing up and serve with soy sauce, pickled ginger and the remaining wasabi paste.

In the foreground:
Hosomaki with Zucchini and Radish Shoots
In the background:
Hosomaki with Avocado and Sesame

Hosomaki with Tuna

● Classic
● Quick

Yields 24 pieces:

5–6 oz fresh tuna fillet
2 scallions
2 tsp wasabi powder
1 roasted nori leaf,
cut into 2 halves
vinegar water
1/2 recipe of pre-prepared
sushi rice (see page 8)
To serve:
soy sauce
pickled ginger

Prep time: 20 minutes

Per piece: 35 calories
2g protein/1g fat/4g
carbohydrates

1 Dab the tuna fillet
dry and cut into strips
about 1/4 inch wide.

2 Clean the scallions
and cut horizontally to
make small rings. Stir
the wasabi powder with
3 tsp water and let it
swell slightly.

3 Using your bamboo
rolling mat (see how
on page 24), form
4 hosomaki rolls
out of the prepared
ingredients.

4 Moisten a sharp knife
with vinegar water, cut
each roll in half and
then cut the halves into
3 pieces of the same
size, cutting either
diagonally or straight.

5 Arrange the sushi
with the cut side facing
up and serve with soy
sauce, pickled ginger
and the remaining
wasabi paste.

TIP!

If you have gotten the
hang of the bamboo
rolling mat, give your
creativity free rein.
Along with the recipes
of classic Japanese sushi
you can combine fish
and seafood with green
vegetables and herbs
however you like. Other
than the taste, the only
important thing is the
combination of colors
in the rolls.

Hosomaki with Surimi and Arugula

● Highly decorative
● Quick

Yields 24 pieces:

4 surimi pieces (see TIP)
2 oz arugula
2 tsp wasabi powder
1 roasted nori leaf,
cut into 2 halves
vinegar water
1/2 recipe of pre-prepared
sushi rice (see page 8)
To serve:
soy sauce
pickled ginger

Prep time: 20 minutes

Per piece: 22 calories
1g protein/<1g fat/4g
carbohydrates

1 Dab the surimi pieces
dry and cut in half.

2 Wash the arugula
and dab dry. Remove
the stalks and chop
coarsely.

3 Stir the wasabi
powder with 3 tsp
water and let it swell
slightly. Using your
bamboo rolling mat
(see how on page 24),
form 4 hosomaki
rolls out of the
prepared ingredients.

4 Moisten a sharp knife
with vinegar water, cut
each roll in half and
then cut the halves into
3 pieces of the same
size, cutting either
diagonally or straight.

5 Arrange the sushi
with the cut side facing
up and serve with soy
sauce, pickled ginger
and the remaining
wasabi paste.

TIPS!

Surimi is imitation crab
meat produced from
fish protein. It is sold
in the form of strips or
"shrimp" tails. Using real
crabmeat would be more
delicious, but also more
expensive. Lobster or
crawfish meat also make
good fillings.

In the foreground:
Hosomaki with Tuna
In the background:
Hosomaki with Surimi
and Arugula

Futomaki with Tofu and Shiitake Mushrooms

● A little more effort
● Vegetarian

Yields 16 pieces:

5 large, dried shiitake mushrooms	
4 tbs soy sauce	
1 tsp sugar	
4 oz hard, smoked tofu	
1 bunch parsley	
1 piece cucumber (about 2 inches long)	
2 tsp wasabi powder	
2 roasted nori leaves	
vinegar water	
1/2 recipe of pre-prepared sushi rice (see page 8)	
To serve:	
soy sauce	
pickled ginger	

Prep time: 40 minutes
plus 30 minutes to soften

Per piece: 61 calories
2g protein/1g fat/13g
carbohydrates

1 Pour 1 cup boiling water over the mushrooms and let them soften for about 30 minutes. Save the water for the next step. Take the mushrooms out, clean them under cold running water, and remove the stalks.

2 Pour the hot water through a fine sieve into a pot. Add the mushrooms, soy sauce and sugar, and simmer for about 10 minutes.

Drain the mushrooms and cut into strips.

3 Cut the tofu lengthwise into strips. Wash the parsley, dab it dry and chop the leaves very coarsely. Peel the cucumber, quarter it lengthwise, remove the seeds and cut into strips. Stir the wasabi powder with 3 tsp water and let it swell slightly.

4 Using your bamboo rolling mat (see how on page 24), form half of the prepared ingredients and a whole nori leaf into one thick futomaki roll.

5 Moisten a sharp knife with vinegar water and cut the roll in half. Then cut the halves into 4 pieces of the same size. Arrange the sushi and serve with soy sauce, pickled ginger and the remaining wasabi paste.

TIP!

Try out this recipe with dried cepes (Boletus edulis), morels or other edible mushrooms.

Futomaki with Omelet, Surimi and Carrots

● A little more effort
● Refined

Yields 16 pieces:

For the omelet:	
2 eggs	
1 tbs mirin	
1 tsp sugar	
soy sauce	
salt	
1 tbs vegetable oil	
For the carrots:	
2 carrots	
5 tbs mirin	
1 tsp sugar	
1 tbs rice vinegar	
salt	
Also:	
2 surimi pieces (see TIP page 28)	
2 tbs sesame seeds	
2 tsp wasabi powder	
2 roasted nori leaves	
vinegar water	
1/2 recipe of pre-prepared sushi rice (see page 8)	
To serve:	
soy sauce	
pickled ginger	

Prep time: 40 minutes

Per piece: 58 calories
2g protein/2g fat/8g
carbohydrates

1 For the omelet: mix the eggs with mirin, sugar, a few drops of soy sauce and a pinch of salt.

2 Heat the oil in a small, non-stick frying pan, put the egg mixture in, and cook it to a hard omelet. Take the omelet out of the pan, let it cool down and cut into strips.

3 Wash the carrots, peel them and cut into strips. Cook the carrot strips in a pot with the mixture made of mirin, sugar, rice vinegar and a pinch of salt for about 1 minute. Allow them to cool down in the broth.

4 Cut the surimi pieces in half lengthwise. Roast the sesame seeds in a pan without oil, until golden: set aside. Stir the wasabi powder with 3 tsp water and let it swell slightly.

5 Using your bamboo rolling mat (see how on page 24), form half of the prepared ingredients and a whole nori leaf into one thick futomaki roll.

6 Moisten a sharp knife with vinegar water and cut the roll in half. Then cut the halves into 4 pieces of the same size.

7 Arrange the sushi decoratively and serve with soy sauce, pickled ginger and the remaining wasabi paste.

VARIATION

For something a little more stylish, try shrimp, lobster or crawfish instead of surimi. You can also refine the omelet with a little pureed fish mixed in.

**In the foreground:
Futomaki with Omelet,
Surimi and Carrots
In the background:
Futomaki with Tofu and
Shiitake Mushrooms**

Futomaki with Radish and Smoked Trout

● Easy to prepare
● Refined

Yields 16 pieces:

4 oz white radish
4 oz smoked trout fillet
4 oz spinach
salt
2 tsp wasabi powder
2 roasted nori leaves
vinegar water
1/2 recipe of pre-prepared sushi rice (see page 8)
To serve:
soy sauce
pickled ginger

Prep time: 40 minutes

Per piece: 43 calories
2g protein/<1g fat/7g carbohydrates

1 Clean and wash the radish and cut with a sharp knife, lengthwise into strips. Cut the trout fillet into strips as well.

2 Wash and blanch the spinach in boiling salt water for 3 minutes. Remove, rinse with cold water and squeeze well. Place the spinach on top of a towel and loosen it up again.

3 Stir the wasabi powder with 3 tsp water and let it swell slightly.

4 Using your bamboo rolling mat (see how on page 24), form half of the prepared ingredients and a whole nori leaf into one thick futomaki roll.

5 Moisten a sharp knife with vinegar water and cut the roll in half. Then cut the halves into 4 pieces of the same size.

6 Arrange the sushi and serve with soy sauce, pickled ginger and the remaining wasabi paste.

Gunkan Maki with Trout Caviar

● Classic
● Easy to prepare

Yields 8 pieces:

2 roasted nori leaves
1 lime
2 tsp wasabi powder
vinegar water
1/2 recipe of pre-prepared sushi rice (see page 8)
3 oz trout caviar
1 piece cucumber (about 1 inch long)
To serve:
soy sauce
pickled ginger

Prep time: 20 minutes

Per piece: 73 calories
3g protein/1g fat/13g carbohydrates

1 Cut each nori leaf into 4 strips about 6 inches x 1 inch.

2 Wash and dry the lime. From the center, cut 4 thin slices and quarter each slice. Squeeze the remaining lime halves into a small bowl. Stir the wasabi powder with 3 tsp of water and let it swell slightly.

3 Moisten your hands with vinegar water and form the sushi rice into 8 oval cakes. Then wrap a strip of nori leaf horizontally around each cake, with the smooth side outwards. Affix the end of the strip with a small amount of vinegar water.

4 Gently press down on the rice from the top. Put a few drops of lime juice and some wasabi on the rice and fill with the caviar. Assemble the rest of the sushi in the same way.

5 Wash the cucumber, cut it in half vertically, remove the seeds, and cut the halves into fine slices. Put some cucumber slices in the caviar as a fan and add a piece of lime. Arrange the sushi and serve with soy sauce, pickled ginger and the remaining wasabi paste.

In the foreground:
Futomaki with White Radish and Smoked Trout
In the background:
Gunkan Maki with Trout Caviar

Gunkan Maki with Smoked Eel Cream

● Classic
● Quick

Yields 8 pieces:

2 oz smoked eel, skinless and boneless
1 tbs sour cream
1 tbs lemon juice
1 tbs mirin
1 bunch chives
2 roasted nori leaves
2 tsp wasabi powder
vinegar water
¹/2 recipe of pre-prepared sushi rice (see page 8)
To serve:
soy sauce
pickled ginger

Prep time: 20 minutes

Per piece: 82 calories
3g protein/2g fat/13g carbohydrates

1 Cut the eel into small pieces and stir it into the sour cream, lemon juice and mirin with a fork until a cream is formed.

2 Wash the chives, dab them dry and cut horizontally into fine rings. Cut each nori leaf into 4 strips about 6 inches x 1 inch. Stir the wasabi powder with 3 tsp water and let it swell slightly.

3 Moisten your hands with vinegar water and form the sushi rice into 8 oval cakes. Wrap each with a strip of nori leaf and affix it with a small amount of vinegar water (see page 32).

4 Gently press down on the rice from the top. Put some wasabi on the rice and fill with the eel cream.

5 Garnish the sushi with the chives, arrange and serve with soy sauce, pickled ginger and the remaining wasabi paste.

> **TIP!**
> Try making other smoked fish into a delicious cream with this recipe.

Gunkan Maki with Mussels

● A little more effort
● Highly decorative

Yields 8 pieces:

about 1 pound mussels, in shell
5 tbs mirin
5 tbs rice vinegar
1 tsp sugar
1 tsp salt
1 piece of ginger about the size of a chestnut
2 roasted nori leaves
2 tsp wasabi powder
vinegar water
¹/2 recipe of pre-prepared sushi rice (see page 8)
To serve:
soy sauce
pickled ginger

Prep time: 20 minutes plus 30 minutes for pickling

Per piece: 70 calories
3g protein/<1g fat/14g carbohydrates

1 Wash the mussels several times in cold water and throw away those which are already open. Boil mirin, rice vinegar, sugar, salt and ginger in a big pot and let the mussels steam in there for about 1 minute, covered. Now throw away the mussels which are still closed, and remove the meat from the rest. Set mussels aside in a stainless steel bowl.

2 Strain the mussel broth through a fine sieve, boil until its volume is reduced by half and pour 2 tbs of it over the mussel meat. Cover, and let the mussels marinate for 30 minutes.

3 Cut each nori leaf into 4 strips about 6 inches x 1 inch. Stir the wasabi powder with 3 tsp water and let it swell slightly.

4 Moisten your hands with vinegar water and form the sushi rice into 8 oval cakes. Wrap each with a strip of nori leaf and affix it with a small amount of vinegar water (see page 32).

5 Gently press down on the rice from the top, put some wasabi on the rice and fill with the mussels. Arrange the sushi and serve with soy sauce, pickled ginger and the remaining wasabi paste.

In the foreground:
Gunkan Maki with Smoked Cream of Eel
In the background:
Gunkan Maki with Mussels

Sushi's Multitude of Forms

There are two aspects to enjoying sushi: it looks wonderful and it tastes great.

Perfectly Shaped

The preceding chapters have given us an idea of how the Japanese chef can make magic with just a few natural ingredients, and come up with delicious and attractive results.

Now it's time to learn other variations of sushi, which are part of the classical tradition but have a unique twist.

Perhaps an original form is reversed, as is the case with ura maki; or a new form is developed through the simplification of a preparation, temaki cones for example. Sometimes the classic sushi ingredients are arranged in a completely new way, and thus a finger-food (sashimi) becomes a small meal in a dish (chirashi). One thing is clear throughout... altered forms of sushi promise new culinary experiences.

Presentation is as impactful as the sushi itself.

Ura Maki... Inside Out

This type of sushi—the Japanese ura maki means "inside-out roll"—is known throughout the rest of the world as the "California" roll. Here the principle of maki-sushi operates in reverse. The nori leaf with the rice on it is turned over, rice-side-down, and the filling placed directly on the leaf. After rolling, the rice is on the outside surrounding the nori leaf, which, in turn surrounds the filling. A happy innovation on the sushi board!

The shape also opens up new opportunities for refinement and decoration. For example, the sushi may be rolled in sesame seeds, herbs or fish eggs.

Temaki: Cone with Filling

With temaki, the nori leaf with the filling is rolled into a cone. Because each cone is formed individually, this technique is a little more elaborate, but the visual effect is well worth the effort. Temaki is actually less work in the kitchen, because there is no rolling with the bamboo mat or cutting rolls into pieces. For a fun alternative to fondue, each guest can compose his or her own temaki according to taste or whim at the table. Nearly anything goes as filling—fish and green vegetables, mussels, shrimp, duck or quail; all are equally ideal for the cone. The ingredients may be raw or steamed, soft or hard.

Temaki is eaten with the fingers; just dip into the soy sauce with wasabi and enjoy. Mmm!

Sashimi: Sushi without the Rice

It might take a little getting used to, but sashimi is the pinnacle of authentic taste. Artistically arranged and decorated, fine cuts of raw fish melt in your mouth. Here, freshness is especially vital. On the day you plan to eat sashimi, go to your fish market and explain that you want to eat the fish raw. Besides salmon and tuna you may want to try fillet of flounder or fresh, day-boat scallops.

Chirashi: Sushi in a Bowl

Particularly in the eastern part of Japan, a form of sushi has been developed which at first sight does not seem to have much in common with traditional sushi: chirashi. Here, slightly spicier rice is served in bowls and covered with the most varied ingredients. There are no recipes or even firm rules. Raw or cooked, fish or greens—the variations are limitless. You may even heat the dishes in steam and serve the result warm as "mushi-sushi.

Rolled the other-way-around or just folded—examples of the varieties of sushi.

Ura Maki with Surimi and Avocado

● Classic
● Highly decorative

Yields 24 pieces:

4 surimi pieces
(see tip on page 28)
1 piece cucumber
(about 4 inches long)
1/2 ripe avocado
1 tbs lemon juice
2 oz wasabi powder
2 roasted nori leaves
vinegar water
1/2 recipe of pre-prepared
sushi rice (see page 8)
1 tbs mayonnaise
4 tbs flying fish roe
(see TIP)

To serve:

soy sauce
pickled ginger

Prep time: 30 minutes

Per piece: 45 calories
1g protein/2g fat/5g
carbohydrates

1 Cut the surimi pieces in half lengthwise. Wash the cucumber, cut in half lengthwise, remove the seeds with a spoon and cut each half of cucumber into 4 strips.

2 Peel the half avocado, cut the flesh lengthwise in 8 strips and brush it with lemon juice. Stir the wasabi powder with 3 tsp water and let it swell slightly.

3 To roll ura maki, cover the bamboo rolling mat with plastic wrap so that the rice does not stick to it.

4 Cut both nori leaves in half and put half of 1 leaf smooth-side down on the bamboo rolling mat, placing one edge of the leaf flush with the edge of the mat. Moisten your hands with vinegar water and spread the sushi rice on the nori leaf.

5 Now turn the leaf and rice over together, so that the rice is now underneath. The best way to do this is to fold the free half of the rolling mat over the rice, and then turn everything over. Carefully lift the other half of the mat—with the film—away from the nori leaf.

6 Spread some mayonnaise with your finger on the nori leaf, and cover the leaf densely with one quarter of the strips of surimi, avocado and cucumber.

7 Form the covered nori leaf, as with hosomaki sushi (see page 24), into a hard, even roll. Coat each roll in roe, making sure that the rice is well-covered with a thin layer. Moisten a sharp knife with vinegar water and cut the roll in half. Then place the two halves side-by-side and cut twice to make 6 pieces of the same size.

8 Continue covering the remaining nori leaves with the rice and other ingredients, rolling them and cutting into pieces of equal size.

9 Arrange the sushi decoratively with the cut side facing up, and serve with soy sauce, pickled ginger and wasabi paste.

> **TIPS!**
>
> By spreading a little of the roe on the rice before turning over the nori leaf, you can also produce the sushi with the fish eggs inside. Instead of serving soy sauce and wasabi separately, try serving soy sauce with some wasabi powder stirred in as a dip.

VARIATION

Substitute the roe with 3 tbs of sesame seeds, roasted in a pan without oil, until golden in color.

Ura Maki with Chopped Tuna

● Easy to prepare
● Highly decorative

Yields 24 pieces:

5–6 oz fresh tuna fillet
2 scallions
2 tsp wasabi powder
1 bunch fresh watercress
2 roasted nori leaves
vinegar water
1/2 recipe of pre-prepared sushi rice (see page 8)
To serve:
soy sauce
pickled ginger

Prep time: 30 minutes

Per piece: 35 calories
2g protein/1g fat/4g carbohydrates

1 Finely chop the tuna fillet. Remove the tops and base of the scallions. Wash them and cut them horizontally into fine rings. Stir the wasabi powder together with 3 tsp water and let it swell slightly. Remove the watercress leaves from the stems with either scissors or by hand and chop coarsely.

2 Cover your bamboo rolling mat with plastic wrap, and place half nori leaf smooth-side down on it. Moisten your hands with vinegar water and spread the sushi rice on the nori leaf (see page 38).

3 Now turn the leaf and rice over together, so that the rice is now underneath. Place some wasabi paste directly on the nori leaf and cover the leaf with a quarter of the tuna and scallions.

4 As with hosomaki sushi (see page 24), form into a hard, even roll. Coat each roll in the watercress leaves and cut into 6 equal pieces (see page 38).

5 Continue covering the remaining nori leaves with the rice and other ingredients, rolling them and cutting into pieces of equal size. Arrange and serve with soy sauce, pickled ginger and the remaining wasabi paste.

Ura Maki with Salmon and Leek

● A little more elaborate
● Highly decorative

Yields 24 pieces:

3 tbs sesame seeds
2 tsp wasabi powder
3–4 oz fresh salmon fillet
1 piece cucumber (about 4 inches long)
1 leek (use only the white part; it should be about 4 inches and as thick as a cucumber—if necessary, use 2 or 3 smaller leeks)
salt
2 roasted nori leaves
vinegar water
1/2 recipe of pre-prepared sushi rice (see page 8)
To serve:
soy sauce
pickled ginger

Prep time: 30 minutes

Per piece: 37 calories
2g protein/1g fat/5g carbohydrates

1 Roast the sesame seeds in a pan without oil until golden in color, and allow to cool. Stir the wasabi powder together with 3 tsp water and let it swell slightly.

2 Dab the salmon fillet dry and cut into strips about 1/2 inch wide. Wash the cucumber, cut in half lengthwise, remove the seeds and cut each half of cucumber into 4 strips.

3 Cut the leek in half lengthwise and wash it. Then cut lengthwise into strips and blanch in boiling salt water for about 1 minute. Remove from the water, rinse with cold water and dab them dry.

4 Cover your bamboo rolling mat with plastic wrap, and place half a nori leaf smooth-side down on it. Moisten your hands with vinegar water and spread the sushi rice on the nori leaf (see page 38).

5 Now turn the leaf and rice over together, so that the rice is now underneath. Place some wasabi paste directly on the nori leaf and cover the leaf densely with a quarter of the leek, cucumber and salmon strips. As with hosomaki sushi (see page 24), form into a hard, even roll. Coat each roll in the sesame seeds and cut into 6 equal pieces (see page 38).

6 Continue covering the remaining nori leaves with the rice and other ingredients, rolling them and cutting into pieces of equal size. Arrange and serve with soy sauce, pickled ginger and the remaining wasabi paste.

VARIATION

Ura Maki with Trout
Peel a large carrot and cut it into strips. Cook in a mixture of 5 tbs mirin, 1 tsp sugar, 1 tbs rice vinegar and a pinch of salt for 1 minute and let the carrot cool down in the liquid. Stir the wasabi paste as described in the recipe. Cut 3–4 oz fresh trout fillet into finger-thick strips. Cover the nori leaves as described with sushi rice, turn over and place some wasabi paste on top of the rice. Cover with carrot strips and trout and form the roll. Coat in trout roe and cut the roll into pieces. Arrange and serve with soy sauce, pickled ginger and the remaining wasabi paste.

In the foreground:
Ura Maki with
Salmon and Leek
In the background:
Ura Maki with
Chopped Tuna

Large Temaki Sushi with Asparagus and Mushrooms

- Highly decorative
- Vegetarian

Yields 8 pieces:

4 asparagus spears
salt
1 tbs rice vinegar
1 tbs mirin
1 pound crimini mushrooms
2 tbs vegetable oil
black pepper
1 tbs soy sauce
1 tbs lemon juice
2 tsp wasabi powder
2 scallions
4 roasted nori leaves
vinegar water
1/2 recipe of pre-prepared sushi rice (see page 8)
To serve:
soy sauce
pickled ginger

Prep time: 30 minutes

Per piece: 102 calories
3g protein/3g fat/15g carbohydrates

1 Wash and trim the asparagus, and trim the lower half of the stalks. Cut them in half lengthwise and across, if necessary. Boil the spears in salt water for 1 minute, rinse with cold water and dry. Then sprinkle with rice vinegar and mirin.

2 Clean the mushrooms and cut them into strips. Heat the oil in a pan and fry the mushrooms until almost all the water has cooked out of them. Spice with salt, pepper, soy sauce and lemon juice.

3 Stir the wasabi powder with 3 tsp water and let it swell slightly. Cut the tops and base from the scallions and cut them into 2 inch pieces, and then into thin strips.

4 Cut the nori leaves in half. Moisten your hands with vinegar water and form the sushi rice into 8 balls.

5 Take the nori leaf with the smooth-side-down in your left hand. Place a rice ball and a bit of wasabi on it. Add 1/8 of the filling and press gently. Fold the lower left corner of the nori leaf to the right and roll the whole leaf into a cone, affixing the leaf with vinegar water.

6 Continue making the temaki in the same way. Arrange decoratively and serve with soy sauce, pickled ginger and the remaining wasabi.

Large Temaki Sushi with Salmon and Avocado

- Classic
- Easy to prepare

Yields 8 pieces:

2 tsp wasabi powder
1/2 ripe avocado
1 tbs lemon juice
1 small zucchini
10–12 oz fresh salmon fillet
4 roasted nori leaves
vinegar water
1/2 recipe of pre-prepared sushi rice (see page 8)
4 tbs salmon roe
To serve:
soy sauce
pickled ginger

Prep time: 30 minutes

Per piece: 175 calories
10g protein/9g fat/13g carbohydrates

1 Stir the wasabi powder with 3 tsp of water and let it swell slightly.

2 Peel the avocado, cut the flesh lengthwise into 8 strips and brush with lemon juice. Wash the zucchini and cut it lengthwise. Dab the salmon fillet dry and cut into 8 strips.

3 Cut the nori leaves in half. Moistening your hands with vinegar water, form the sushi rice into 8 regular balls.

4 Take the nori leaf with the smooth-side down in your left hand, place a rice ball on the left side and put some wasabi paste on it. Put 1/8 of the filling on it and press down gently.

5 Now fold the lower left corner of the nori leaf all the way to the right and roll the whole leaf into a pointed cone. Affix the nori leaf with vinegar water.

6 Continue making the other temaki sushi in the same way. Spread some salmon roe on each cone. Arrange the sushi decoratively and serve with soy sauce, pickled ginger and the wasabi paste.

In the foreground:
Large Temaki Sushi with Salmon and Avocado
In the background:
Large Temaki Sushi with Asparagus and Mushrooms

Small Temaki Sushi with Shrimp, Cucumber and Radish

● Highly decorative
● A little more expensive

Yields 16 pieces:

2 tsp wasabi powder
8 oz shrimp, cooked and peeled
1 tbs mirin
1 tbs lemon juice
2 tbs mayonnaise
1 piece cucumber (about 4 inches long)
1 piece white radish (about 4 inches long)
4 roasted nori leaves
vinegar water
1/2 recipe of pre-prepared sushi rice (see page 8)
4 tbs radish shoots
To serve:
soy sauce
pickled ginger

Prep time: 40 minutes

Per piece: 57 calories
3g protein/2g fat/7g carbohydrates

1 Stir the wasabi powder with 3 tsp of water and let it swell slightly.

2 Mix the shrimp with mirin, lemon juice and mayonnaise. Wash the cucumber, quarter it lengthwise and remove the seeds. Remove the tops and base of the radish and wash it. Cut the cucumber and radish lengthwise in fine strips.

3 Quarter the nori leaves and take one quarter with the smooth-side down in your left hand. Moisten your right hand with vinegar water, place some sushi rice on the left side of the nori leaf and put some wasabi paste on it.

4 Place some of the filling on top of the rice and press gently. Now roll the nori leaf into a pointed cone and affix with some vinegar water (see page 42).

5 Continue making the temaki sushi in this manner. Decorate each one with radish shoots and serve with soy sauce, pickled ginger and the remaining wasabi paste.

Small Temaki Sushi with Snow Peas and Mackerel

● Traditional
● A little more effort

Yields 16 pieces:

2 tsp wasabi powder
5–6 oz fresh mackerel fillet
3 tbs salt
2 tbs lemon juice
5 tbs rice vinegar
5 tbs mirin
2 tsp sugar
4 oz snow peas
4 roasted nori leaves
vinegar water
1/2 recipe of pre-prepared sushi rice (see page 8)
To serve:
soy sauce
pickled ginger

Prep time: 40 minutes plus 4 to 6 hours for pickling

Per piece: 55 calories
3g protein/2g fat/7g carbohydrates

1 Stir the wasabi powder with 3 tsp of water and let it swell slightly.

2 Dab the mackerel fillet dry and remove any bones. Rub the mackerel with 3 tbs salt and place covered in a cool spot for 3 to 5 hours. Then rinse off the salt with cold water, and dry the fillet again.

3 Stir the lemon juice with rice vinegar, mirin and sugar until the sugar has dissolved. Place the fish fillet in a flat dish, cover with the marinade and let stand for about 1 hour, turning occasionally.

4 Then dry the marinated mackerel fillet and peel away the skin. Cut the fish with a sharp knife diagonally into 16 pieces as evenly as possible.

5 Clean the snow peas and wash them. Blanch in boiling salt water for 2 minutes and rinse immediately with cold water. Dab dry and cut lengthwise into strips.

6 Quarter the nori leaves and take one quarter with the smooth-side down in your left hand. Moisten your right hand with vinegar water, place some sushi rice on the left side of the nori leaf and put some wasabi paste on it.

7 Place a piece of mackerel and some of the snow peas on top of the rice and press gently. Now roll the nori leaf into a pointed cone and affix with some vinegar water (see page 42).

(see page 42).

8 Continue making the temaki sushi in this manner. Arrange the sushi and serve with soy sauce, pickled ginger and the remaining wasabi paste.

On the left:
Small Temaki Sushi with
Snow Peas and Mackerel
On the right:
Small Temaki Sushi
with Shrimp, Cucumber
and Radish

Sashimi with Perch and Scallops

- A little more effort
- Highly decorative

For 4 people:

3–4 oz seaweed
2 oz white radish
1 piece cucumber (about 4 inches long)
about 1 pound fresh wolf perch fillet
8 scallops (only the white flesh; see tip on page 20)
1 lemon
4 tsp wasabi powder
2 roasted nori leaves
4 cooked shrimp, in the shell
4 tbs salmon roe
To serve:
soy sauce
pickled ginger

Prep time: 30 minutes

Per piece: 126 calories
25g protein/2g fat/3g
carbohydrates

1 Blanch the seaweed for about 2 minutes in boiling water. Rinse with cold water and drain.

2 Clean the radish, peel and cut lengthwise into very fine strips. Wash the cucumber, cut in half lengthwise, remove the seeds with a small spoon and cut the halves horizontally in thin slices.

3 Cut the wolf perch fillet across the fiber and on a slight diagonal in pieces about ½ inch wide. Cut the flesh of the scallops into thin slices. Stir the wasabi powder with 2 tbs water and let it swell slightly.

4 Wash the lemon with water, dry and cut inyo thin slices. Cut the nori leaves into strips. Peel the shrimp without removing the tail.

5 Arrange the seaweed, radish strips and cucumber slices decoratively with the fish strips, scallop slices and one shrimp each on four flat plates or classic sushi boards. Add to each: 1 tsp wasabi paste, some lemon slices and nori strips, and 1 tbs salmon roe. Serve with soy sauce and pickled ginger.

Sashimi with Oysters, Tuna and Salmon

- Easy to prepare
- A little more expensive

For 4 people:

1 carrot
3–4 oz white radish
1 dried chili pepper
8 oz fresh salmon fillet
8 oz fresh tuna fillet
8 oysters
1 lime
2 roasted nori leaves
4 tsp wasabi powder
To serve:
soy sauce
pickled ginger

Prep time: 30 minutes

Per piece: 242 calories
23g protein/15g fat/4g
carbohydrates

1 Clean the carrot, peel and cut lengthwise as thinly as possible.

2 Clean the radish, peel and bore a small hole in the center. Put the chili pepper in the hole, then grate the whole thing very finely. Squeeze the liquid out of the grated radish and form 4 small, loose cakes with it.

3 Dab the salmon and tuna fillets dry, and cut across the fibers, on a slight diagonal in pieces about ½ inch wide. Open the oysters, separate the meat from the shell and leave resting in the lower shell.

4 Wash the lime with water, dry and cut into thin slices. Cut the nori leaves into strips. Stir the wasabi powder with 2 tbs water and let it swell slightly.

5 Arrange the carrot strips, radish cakes, and salmon and tuna strips decoratively with the oysters, lime slices, wasabi paste and the nori strips on four plates or sushi boards. Serve with soy sauce and pickled ginger.

In the foreground:
Sashimi with Oysters,
Tuna and Salmon
In the background:
Sashimi with Wolf Perch

Chirashi Sushi with Salmon

● Classic
● Highly decorative

For 4 people:

2 tbs sesame seeds
3–4 oz spinach
salt
1 tbs lemon juice
8 oz bamboo shoots (canned)
2 carrots
1 tbs sugar
2 tbs soy sauce
2 tbs mirin
2 tbs rice vinegar
about 1 pound fresh salmon fillet
1 recipe of pre-prepared, warm sushi rice (page 8)
4 slices lotus root (canned)
3–4 oz pickled ginger
4 tsp wasabi powder
To serve:
soy sauce

Prep time: 30 minutes

Per piece: 519 calories
29g protein/18g fat/61g
carbohydrates

1 Roast the sesame seeds in a pan without oil until golden in color. Set aside.

2 Sort the spinach, wash and blanch very briefly in boiling salt water. Rinse with cold water, squeeze and then loosen it again and mix with the lemon juice and sesame seeds.

3 Drain the bamboo shoots and cut into thin slices. Clean and peel the carrots, and cut lengthwise in strips. Boil 1/2 cup water with sugar, soy sauce, mirin and rice vinegar and cook the carrot strips in this liquid for 1 minute. Allow carrots to cool in the broth, then remove and dab them dry.

4 Dab the salmon fillet dry and cut across the fiber on a slight diagonal into pieces about 1/4 inch wide. Stir the wasabi powder with 2 tbs water and let it swell slightly.

5 Portion the warm sushi rice into four dishes and arrange the spinach, bamboo shoots, carrots and salmon pieces on it with slices of lotus root, ginger and the wasabi paste. Serve with soy sauce.

Chirashi Sushi with Smoked Fish

● Easy to prepare
● Refined

For 4 people:

1 bunch radishes
3–4 oz cucumber
1 bunch chives
3–4 oz smoked trout fillet
3–4 oz smoked salmon fillet
3–4 oz smoked eel fillet
1 recipe of pre-prepared, warm sushi rice (page 8)
3–4 oz pickled ginger
4 tsp wasabi powder
To serve:
soy sauce

Prep time: 30 minutes

Per piece: 458 calories
23g protein/15g fat/55g
carbohydrates

1 Remove the tops and base of the radishes, wash them and slice thinly. Wash the cucumber, cut in half lengthwise, remove the seeds and cut the halves crosswise into thin slices.

2 Wash the chives, dab them dry and chop finely.

3 Cut the smoked fish fillets across the fiber on a slight diagonal into pieces about 1/4 inch wide. Stir the wasabi powder with 2 tbs water and let it swell slightly.

4 Portion the warm sushi rice into four dishes and arrange the smoked fish, radish and cucumber slices on it with the pickled ginger and the wasabi paste. Sprinkle the sushi with the chives and serve with soy sauce.

TIP!

Of course, this recipe tastes good with any type of smoked fish— preferably without bones. Never combine smoked fish with fresh, raw fish. The intense aroma of the smoke will blanket the delicate flavor of the fish.

In the foreground:
Chirashi Sushi with Salmon
In the background:
Chirashi Sushi with a
Variety of Smoked Fish

New Sushi

The idea of sushi has been spread throughout the world not only by the Japanese themselves, but also by tourists returning from the land of the Rising Sun. Having once sampled the countless varieties of sushi, visitors found they no longer wanted to live without these delicacies.

Sushi Fusion

The passage of time, the interplay of various cultures, and new possibilities for ingredients have given birth to many new varieties of sushi worldwide. Many of these culinary "inventions" have now made their way back to Japan.

Meat, or even cheese instead of fish; herbs in place of green vegetables—New Sushi is a delicious combination of both Asian and European cuisines.

Sushi as a Creative Endeavor

As a creative chef, you may well find yourself ultimately dissatisfied with a range of ingredients limited to rice, seaweed, green vegetables and raw fish. Why not combine the multitude of Western cuisine with this Far East foundation? In this way you can find deliciously new, unexplored landscapes of taste.

For example, use meat for sushi filling. After the initial surprise, you'll see it's a perfect complement to the other ingredients.

Even such a small difference as using cooked fish instead of raw fish can give the sushi an entirely different taste without altering the other ingredients.

Play with the Form

What begins with the ingredients continues with the form: sushi in a circle or semicircle can delight the eye just as much as a rectangle or oval. Rolls can be wrapped in a variety of lettuce leaves as opposed to nori.

With a basic grounding in the classic techniques, many ideas to transform classic sushi into New Sushi come as you prepare the traditional forms. It can even begin with the simple act of cutting the rolls: why not try cutting them on a diagonal instead of straight? With this basic adjustment... New Sushi is born!

Play with the Content

As is always the case with the art of cooking—be it baking, confectionery, salads, or any other realm—true freedom for innovation and imagination is gained only by practice, practice and more practice. There are no fixed rules, no manual; in the game of improvisation there are only ideas.

Create interesting aromas using shellfish, surimi pieces or fish flavored with rare herbs. Replacing fish with meat opens entirely new arenas of taste. Try duck breast, lamb, beef or chicken. You

can use out-of-season vegetables for your sushi creations by cooking and pickling them—for example sweet-and-sour, pickled pumpkin.

And try sushi...warm! It's not such a strange idea—and quite covenient when the ingredients are cooked anyway.

The basic idea is be adventurous! Try whatever tastes good, and look out for unusual combinations. If you find that some ingredients don't blend together as well as you had hoped—just go on and try something else!

Salmon Cone with Honey Mustard

● Easy to prepare
◐ Refined

Yields 16 pieces:

1 tbs spicy mustard
1 tbs traditional mustard (e.g. Dijon)
1 tbs honey
1 tbs white wine vinegar
1 tbs vegetable oil
6 oz marinated salmon
1/2 recipe of pre-prepared sushi rice (see page 8)
To garnish:
a few sprigs of dill
lotus root slices (canned)

Prep time: 30 minutes

Per piece: 61 calories
3g protein/2g fat/7g carbohydrates

1 Stir the two types of mustard together with the honey, vinegar and oil to a smooth consistency.

2 Cut the salmon as evenly as possible into 16 slices.

3 Put a piece of plastic wrap into an egg cup (or any very small bowl), and put a slice of salmon in it. Put a dollop of the honey mustard mixture on the salmon, and fill the cup with sushi rice.

4 Press the rice down gently. If any of the salmon hangs out, either fold it back in, or trim it and enjoy as a quick appetizer.

5 Now turn over the egg cup onto a plate and take off the plastic wrap.

6 Go on making the rest of the salmon cones, arrange them on a plate, and garnish the plate with the dill and lotus roots.

VARIATION

Try changing the colors: the rice can be colored red with beet juice, and instead of salmon you can use smoked halibut.

Gunkan Maki with Oysters and Sweet Lime Mayonnaise

● Highly decorative
◐ Quick

Yields 8 pieces:

8 small oysters
1 lime
2 tbs mayonnaise
1 tbs yogurt
black pepper
2 roasted nori leaves
vinegar water
1/2 recipe of pre-prepared sushi rice (see page 8)

Prep time: 20 minutes

Per piece: 90 calories
2g protein/4g fat/13g carbohydrates

1 Open the oysters, separate the meat from the shell, and allow it to drain.

2 Wash the lime, dry it, remove about half of the peel and cut the peel into very fine strips. Squeeze the rest of the lime, and mix two tbs of the juice with the mayonnaise, yogurt and half of the lime peel. Season with black pepper.

3 Cut each of the nori leaves into four strips about 6 inches x 1 inch. Moisten your hands with vinegar water and form the sushi rice into

8 oval cakes. Wrap each with a strip of nori leaf and affix with vinegar water. (see page 32).

4 Top the rice with an oyster and press down gently. Add a dollop of the sweet lime mayonnaise mixture, and garnish the sushi with the remaining strips of lime peel.

> **TIP!**
>
> For those who find raw oysters a little too much, they also make a very nice filling when cooked. Boil 1/2 cup white wine with 1/2 cup fish broth and poach the oysters for 1 minute, or hold them in a sieve just above the broth and let them steam for 2 minutes.

In the foreground:
Gunkan Maki with Oysters and Sweet Lime Mayonnaise
In the background:
Salmon Cone with Honey Mustard

Ura Maki with Chicken and Crab

● Easy to prepare
● A little more expensive

Yields 24 pieces:

4 oz cooked fillet of chicken breast
4 oz crabmeat (canned)
1/2 bunch chives
2 tbs mayonnaise
2 tsp wasabi powder
2 roasted nori leaves, cut into halves
Vinegar water
1/2 recipe of pre-prepared sushi rice (see page 8)
To serve:
soy sauce
pickled ginger

Prep time: 30 minutes

Per piece: 39 calories
2g protein/1g fat/4g carbohydrates

1 Cut the chicken into strips. Wash the crab, dry it, and chop it finely.

2 Wash and dry the chives, and chop finely. Mix with the mayonnaise.

3 Stir the wasabi powder together with 3 tsp of water and let it swell slightly.

4 Cover a bamboo rolling mat with plastic wrap, and place half a nori leaf smooth-side down on it. Moisten your hands with vinegar water and spread the sushi rice on the leaf (see page 38).

5 Now turn over the nori and rice together, so that the rice is now underneath. Place some chive mayonnaise on top of the nori leaf and cover the leaf with a quarter of the chicken and crab.

6 As in hosomaki sushi (see page 24), form into a hard, even roll and cut into 6 equal pieces (see page 38).

7 Continue covering the remaining nori leaves with the rice and other ingredients, rolling them and cutting into pieces of equal size. Arrange and serve with soy sauce, pickled ginger and the remaining wasabi paste.

Ura Maki with Black Rice and Cuttlefish

● A little more elaborate
● Highly decorative

Yields 24 pieces:

3 tbs sesame seeds
2 tsp wasabi powder
4 sprigs cilantro
5-6 oz fresh, cleaned cuttlefish tubes
2 roasted nori leaves
vinegar water
1/2 recipe of pre-prepared sushi rice (see page 8). Ask your fish market for a small bag of cuttlefish (or squid) ink to color the cooking water black.
To serve:
soy sauce
pickled ginger

Prep time: 30 minutes

Per piece: 31 calories
2g protein/1g fat/4g carbohydrates

1 Roast the sesame seeds in a pan without oil until golden in color, and allow them to cool. Stir the wasabi powder together with 3 tsp water and let it swell slightly.

2 Wash and dry the cilantro, and remove the leaves from the stalk.

3 Cut the cuttlefish in half lengthwise, wash it and dab it dry. Then cut it lengthwise into thin strips.

4 Cover a bamboo rolling mat with plastic wrap and place half of a nori leaf smooth-side down on it. Moisten your hands with vinegar water and spread the sushi rice on the leaf (see page 38).

5 Now turn over the nori and rice together, so that the rice is now underneath. Place some wasabi paste on top of the nori leaf and cover the leaf with a quarter of the cuttlefish strips and the cilantro.

6 As in hosomaki sushi (see page 24), form into a hard, even roll. Coat each roll in the sesame seeds and cut into 6 equal pieces (see page 38).

7 Continue covering the remaining nori leaves with the rice and other ingredients, rolling them, covering with sesame seeds and cutting into pieces of equal size. Arrange and serve with soy sauce, pickled ginger and the remaining wasabi paste.

VARIATION

Ura Maki with Monkfish and Saffron Rice

Prepare 1/2 recipe sushi rice, adding several stems of saffron halfway through the cooking. Dry a 5–6 oz fillet of monkfish with a clean kitchen towel, and cut it into thin strips. Heat 1 tbs of olive oil in a non-stick frying pan, add one clove of minced garlic to it and fry lightly. Add the monkfish, fry for one minute, remove and set it on a paper towel. Prepare the wasabi paste as described in the recipe above. Repeating the process 4 times. Place one half of a roasted nori leaf onto the wrapped rolling mat and spread the sushi rice on it. Turn the leaf and rice over together. Place some wasabi paste on top of the nori leaf and cover with a quarter of the fish strips. Roll the sushi, coat it with black sesame seeds and cut it. Serve with soy sauce, pickled ginger and the remaining wasabi paste.

In the foreground:
Ura Maki with
Chicken and Crab
In the background:
Ura Maki with Black
Rice and Cuttlefish

Hosomaki Caprese

- Refined
- Vegetarian

Yields 24 pieces:

2 or 3 fully ripe tomatoes
(about 7 oz)
4 – 5 oz Mozzarella cheese
(preferably buffalo
Mozzarella or other
soft variety)
1 bunch basil leaves
(about 24)
2 tsp wasabi powder
2 roasted nori leaves,
cut in half
vinegar water
1/2 recipe of pre-prepared
sushi rice (see page 8)
To serve:
Balsamic vinegar

Prep time: 20 minutes

Per piece: 33 calories
2g protein/1g fat/4g
carbohydrates

1 Remove the core
from each of the
tomatoes. Make
two small cuts on
the bottom of the
tomatoes, which
form an "x". Place
the tomatoes briefly
in boiling water until
the peel is about to
fall off. Cool them in
cold water, peel them
starting from the loose
ends of the "x" and
quarter them. Remove
the seeds and liquid
and cut the meat
into strips.

2 Let the mozzarella
drain in a colander.
Cut it into thin slices,
and the slices into
thin strips. Wash the
basil leaves and dab
them dry.

3 Stir the wasabi
powder with 3 tsp
water and let it
swell slightly.

4 Using your bamboo
rolling mat, form 4
hosomaki rolls from the
prepared ingredients
(see how on page 24).

5 Moisten a sharp
knife with vinegar
water, cut each roll
in half and then cut
the halves into 3
pieces of the same
size, cutting either
diagonally or straight.

6 Arrange the sushi
decoratively with the
cut side facing up and
serve with balsamic
vinegar instead of
soy sauce.

Nigiri Sushi with Fillet of Beef

- Easy to prepare
- Refined

Yields 8 pieces:

5 – 6 oz fillet of beef
(preferably organic)
4 tbs black peppercorns
2 tsp wasabi powder
vinegar water
1/2 recipe of pre-prepared
sushi rice (see page 8)
To serve:
soy sauce

Prep time: 30 minutes

Per piece: 83 calories
5g protein/1g fat/13g
carbohydrates

1 Dab the fillet dry and
cut with a sharp knife
into 8 pieces about
1 x 2 inches each.

2 Crush the pepper-
corns with a mortar
and pestle, or squash
them with a wide
knife on a board.

3 Stir the wasabi
powder together with
3 tsp water and let it
swell slightly. Put a
little of the resulting
wasabi paste onto the
middle of each piece
of meat.

4 Moisten your hands
with vinegar water
and form the sushi
rice into 8 oval cakes.

5 Take a piece of beef
in your left hand, with
the wasabi side facing
up. Place a rice cake
on top and press down
with your thumb.

6 Turn the sushi over,
and press first from
above and then from
the sides to obtain a
regular shape (see on
page 12).

7 Assemble and form
the rest of the sushi in
the same way. Sprinkle
the peppercorns on
the sushi and arrange.
Serve with soy sauce
and the remaining
wasabi paste.

In the foreground:
Nigiri Sushi with
Fillet of Beef
In the background:
Hosomaki Caprese

Futomaki with Herring, Cucumber and Radish

● Easy to prepare
● Refined

Yields 16 pieces:

4 oz herring
1 piece of cucumber
(about 4 inches long)
4 oz white radish
1 zucchini
2 tsp wasabi powder
2 roasted nori leaves
vinegar water
1/2 recipe of pre-prepared
sushi rice (see page 8)
To serve:
soy sauce
pickled ginger

Prep time: 40 minutes

Per piece: 49 calories
2g protein/2g fat/7g
carbohydrates

1 Clean the herring with cold water, dab dry and cut in strips 1/2 inch thick.

2 Peel the cucumber, quarter lengthwise, remove the seeds with a tsp and cut into strips. Remove the tops and base of the radish and zucchini. Wash them and cut both into strips with a sharp knife.

3 Stir the wasabi powder with 3 tsp water and let it swell slightly.

4 Using your bamboo rolling mat, form half of the prepared ingredients and a whole nori leaf into one thick futomaki roll (see how on page 24).

5 Moisten a sharp knife with vinegar water and cut the roll in half. Then cut the halves into 4 pieces of the same size.

6 Arrange the sushi decoratively and serve with soy sauce, pickled ginger and the remaining wasabi paste.

Large Temaki Sushi with Duck Breast and Mirin Plums

● A little more elaborate
● A little more expensive

Yields 8 pieces:

1 duck breast
(about 8–9 oz)
1 tbs sesame oil
1 tbs soy sauce
black pepper
8 pitted prunes
4 oz mirin
5 tbs rice vinegar
1 tsp wasabi powder
2 scallions
4 roasted nori leaves
vinegar water
1/2 recipe of pre-prepared
sushi rice (see page 8)
To serve:
soy sauce
pickled ginger

Prep time: 30 minutes

Per piece: 181 calories
7g protein/7g fat/18g
carbohydrates

1 Remove the skin from the duck breast and cut the meat into thin strips. Heat the oil in a non-stick frying pan and fry the duck at very high heat for about 2 minutes. Add the soy sauce and a pinch of pepper.

2 Quarter the prunes lengthwise and boil them in a pot with the mirin and the rice vinegar. Leave the prunes in this broth for about 30 minutes, then take them out and dry them with a clean towel.

3 Stir the wasabi powder with 3 tsp of water and let it swell slightly. Cut off the tops and base of the scallions, wash them and cut them diagonally.

4 Cut the nori leaves in half. Moistening your hands with vinegar water, form the sushi rice into 8 regular balls.

5 Take the nori leaf with the smooth side down in your left hand. Place a rice ball on the left side and put some wasabi paste on it. Put an eighth of the filling on it and press.

6 Now fold the lower left corner of the nori leaf all the way to the right and roll the whole leaf into a pointed cone. Affix the nori with a small amount of vinegar water.

7 Go on making the other temaki sushi in the same way. Arrange the sushi decoratively and serve with soy sauce, pickled ginger and the remaining wasabi paste.

TIP!

Instead of duck breast you can also slice and fry beef, pork—even ostrich.

In the foreground:
Large Temaki Sushi with Duck Breast and mirin plums
In the background:
Futomaki with Herring, Cucumber and Radish

Small Temaki Sushi with Fillet of Lamb and Savoy Cabbage

- A little more elaborate
- A little more expensive

Yields 16 pieces:

2 tsp wasabi powder	
1 piece cucumber (about 4 inches long)	
4 light green leaves of savoy cabbage	
salt	
1 pound fillet of lamb	
1 tbs olive oil	
2 tbs white wine	
4 roasted nori leaves	
vinegar water	
1/2 recipe of pre-prepared sushi rice (see page 8)	
black pepper	
To serve:	
soy sauce	

Prep time: 40 minutes

Per piece: 65 calories
6g protein/2g fat/7g
carbohydrates

1 Stir the wasabi powder with 3 tsp of water and let it swell slightly. Wash the cucumber, quarter it lengthwise and remove the seeds. Cut lengthwise in fine strips.

2 Blanch the savoy cabbage leaves in boiling salt water for about 3 minutes. Rinse under cold water, remove the stalks, dry and cut the leaves into strips.

3 Cut the fillet of lamb into strips and fry in very hot olive oil for about 1 minute. Add the white wine and simmer until the lamb is fully cooked.

4 Quarter the nori leaves and take one quarter with the smooth side down in your left hand. Moisten your right hand with vinegar water, place some sushi rice on the left side of the nori leaf and put some wasabi paste on it.

5 Place some of the strips of lamb, cucumber and savoy cabbage on top of the rice and press gently. Roll the nori leaf into a pointed cone and affix with a small amount of vinegar water (see page 42).

6 Continue making the temaki sushi until the ingredients are all used. Sprinkle each one with some freshly ground pepper and serve with soy sauce and the remaining wasabi paste.

Hosomaki with Beetroot and Arugula

- Highly decorative
- Vegetarian

Yields 24 pieces:

5–6 oz red beet, cooked and peeled	
2 oz arugula	
2 tsp wasabi powder	
2 roasted nori leaves, cut in half	
vinegar water	
1/2 recipe of pre-prepared sushi rice (see page 8), half of the cooking water should be substituted with beet juice	
To serve:	
soy sauce	
pickled ginger	

Prep time: 20 minutes

Per piece: 24 calories
1g protein/<1g fat/5g
carbohydrates

1 Cut the beet into strips about 1/4 inch thick

2 Wash and dry the arugula. Remove the stalks and chop the leaves coarsely.

3 Stir the wasabi powder with 3 tsp water and let it swell slightly.

4 Using your bamboo rolling mat (see how on page 24), form 4 hosomaki rolls out of the beet and the arugula.

5 Moisten a sharp knife with vinegar water, cut each roll in half and then cut the halves into 3 pieces of the same size.

6 Arrange the sushi with the cut side facing up and serve with soy sauce, pickled ginger and the remaining wasabi paste.

In the foreground:
Small Temaki Sushi
with Fillet of Lamb
and Savoy Cabbage
In the background:
Hosomaki with
Beetroot and Arugula

Credits

Published originally under the title Sushi © 2001 Gräfe
and Unzer Publishers GmbH, Munich.
English translation for the U.S. market © 2002, Silverback
Books, Inc.

Food Editor: Jonathan Silverman
Editor: Christine Wehling
Layout, typography and cover design: Heinz Kraxenberger
Setting and production: Verlagssatz Lingner
Production: Helmut Giersberg
Typesetting and production: Patty Holden and Helmut
Giersberg
Cover photo: Michael Brauner
Photos: Kai Mewes
Food Styling: Akos Neuberger
Reproduction: Repro Schmidt
ISBN 1-930603-22-3
Printed in Hong Kong

Andreas Furtmayr
converted his hobby into his profession: he writes and
translates cookbooks, owns a wine shop in Munich, and
organizes parties and events, taking charge of the
catering and stationing himself at the stove. What this
passionate cook and gourmet enjoys most is spoiling his
guests: often with sushi.

Kai Mewes
is a freelance food photographer in Munich and works
for publishers and advertisers. His studio has an inte-
grated kitchen, and is located close to Viktualien market.
The atmospheric photos are expressions of his ideal: a
unification of photography with culinary pleasure.

Translated by:
Peter Stegemann
Andrew Blake
HTS

ABBREVIATIONS	
oz	= ounce
tsp	= teaspoon
tbs	= tablespoon